Soft Encounters. The Definitive Guide To Diving
With Grey Seals

Thanks to Jane for help with the editing and to Micky and Ben for the rest.

The what, the where, the when and the how

The what

I work as a scuba diving instructor and commercial dive boat skipper. My office is the Farne islands in Northumberland where I have dived on and off for the past 20 years, the Farnes remain one of my favourite places to dive in all of the world.

One of the greatest draws for divers visiting the Farne islands are the grey seals. The UK plays host to almost half of the world population of these playful creatures and the Farne island colony is one of the largest numbering around 6000 individuals.

Unlike any other colony in the world the Farne Island grey seals are not fazed by seeing divers in the water, people have been diving around the islands since the 1960s and there have been trip boats taking tourists out to see the seals for over 100 years, because of this every generation of grey seals that live around the islands are used to seeing human beings both in and out of the water, this is why the Farne islands are the best place on earth to dive with grey seals.

There were over 3000 seal pups born around the islands in the 2020 season, around 2700 in 2019 and over 2500 in 2018. although the numbers are impressive it has to be remembered that only around 50% of these pups will survive their first year.

The pups weigh around 15kg at birth and rapidly put on

weight until they are weaned at between 4 and 5 weeks, a healthy pup will weigh around 50 kg when it is weaned and will resemble a large white ball of fluff.

The seal pups are very vulnerable at this stage in their lives as they still have their white coat which provides very little protection against the cold North sea. The seal pup will stay on the beach surviving on its excess fat and calorie reserves while it moults its white coat, allowing its adult grey coat to grow through.

Over a period of three to four weeks the seal pup will lose weight and slim down to a healthy 25 kg or so, it will receive no further sustenance from its mother and it will shed its white coat. The young seal will then head out to sea to learn its trade. The grey seal pup recieves no instruction in hunting and survival from the parent seal but instead relies completely on instincts and genetic memory.

After six to twelve months the seal pup will make its way back to the islands. From August onwards you will begin to see small groups of young seals gathered together as well as individual youngsters clinging to the outskirts of larger groups of adults, these small seals are the pups from the previous season that have returned to establish their place in the colony.

The grey seal female or cow seal will reach sexual maturity at between two and three years old while the grey seal male or bull will become mature at between five and seven years. In the meantime these young seals will spend their time hunting and playing and generally making mischief.

A diver in the water is seen as a curiosity or plaything and is of great interest to the adolescent seal. The young seals will take turns at sneaking up on the diver, initially from behind as they love to nibble the divers fins. The young seals will get increasingly bold as the game progresses, where more than one seal is involved in the game the seals will tend to egg each other on and these encounters can often end in a full scale diver mugging.

It's not only the adolescents that are interested in the divers however, the adult cow seals are also attracted to the divers but for different reasons.

From September through to October and into November is the busiest period of the seals calendar, it is not only pupping time but is also breeding season for the grey seals. The bull seals that have been absent for the greater part of the year have made their way back to the islands to choose their territory and divide up the females. The majority of the bull seals head over from a secluded beach on the mainland where they spend most of the year. Very few adult bulls spend the full season around the islands, preferring their own company at their private 'boys club'

Needless to say, a diver dressed head to toe in black neoprene and packing a few extra pounds can be seen by the cow seal as something of a catch.

The cow seal is one of the few mammals that can fertilise her egg while still being pregnant, she can store a fertilised egg until she gives birth then the fertilised egg will move into the womb where the fetus will grow for the 10 months gestation period and the cycle begins again.

As her time gets closer the cow seals maternal instincts as well as instinct to breed attracts her to both the bull seals and any divers that happen to be in the water.

The bull seal is a territorial fellow and will warn other bull seals and divers that the females in his territory are not available. He does this with a series of loud grunts which are clearly audible under water, you wont always see the bull seal but you will certainly hear him. If the grunting doesn't work the bull seal will clap, this clap sounds to the diver like a small series of explosions. It is very loud and it's been likened to the sound of underwater construction or dynamite fishing, it's the bull seals way of saying listen to me! I'm big and scary! Stay away from my ladies! The clap was first documented right here in the Farne islands by my good friend Ben Burville. Prior to this, experts believed the sound to be another vocalisation like the grunts even though the clapping has been recorded in other pinnipeds such as the walrus.

The adult bull seal will rarely interact with divers but when he does it can be quite intimidating and I would always advise against it for the inexperienced seal diver.

There are some major differences worth pointing out between interactions with young adolescent seals and adult females. As mentioned previously the young adolescents will follow the divers along the reef nibbling at their fins and any loose equipment that may be accessible, they will get increasingly bold, eventually approaching the diver from the front, often allowing a belly rub or fist bump. The adult pregnant female seal on the other hand will tend to cling onto the diver usually on the leg or cylinder with her front flippers, if you stay with her on the seabed she might cuddle, allow belly rubs and often hold hands with the diver.

There are tricks and techniques for getting the best out of these encounters and that is what this book is all about. The chapters of this book are titled the what, the when, the where and the how and by reading through chapter by chapter the diver wanting to interact with grey seals will gain a thorough knowledge of the best ways to make this happen.

All grey seal encounters happen on the grey seals terms. This is the most important thing to remember, we are entering the grey seals environment uninvited and we will usually be made very welcome but If the seals don't want to play there is absolutely nothing you can do to force an interaction. This book is titled Soft Encounters, the definition of which is that we cause no stress or harm to the seals and that the seals get as much out of the experience as the diver does.

The grey seal is a wild animal, it is the U.K.'s biggest predator and as such should be afforded respect, an adult cow seal will weigh up so 150kg and measure over a meter and a half in length. She has a small doglike head and is usually mottled in shades of grey, white and black. The male on the other hand can easily reach 350kg and measure in excess of two meters, he is much darker in colour, often appearing black underwater. His head is much bigger with a hooked nose much like a brown bear, in fact the grey seals closest land relative is the brown bear and if provoked the bite pressure of an adult male is comparable with that of the bear so great care must be taken when diving with these creatures.

As a rule, while they are in the water the grey seal is a friendly mischievous dive buddy, the seal can move at speeds in excess of twenty miles per hour and change direction quicker than we can blink. She can hold her breath for up to twenty minutes and dive to depths of three hundred meters on that one breath.

We on the other hand can only bimble along the reef at a sedate two or three miles per hour. Sometimes less depending on the current. We can change direction 'eventually' and in some cases we can breathe a full tank of air in twenty minutes, its no wonder the seal feels safe to approach and investigate the diver.

It's rare for a diver to be injured by a seal but not unheard of. Usually injuries are incurred due to bad decisions on the divers part, reaching out for an unsolicited stroke, cornering or surprising the seal or worst of all scaring the seals into the water while they are hauled out resting.

Many people compare the grey seal to a Labrador dog. Admittedly they do look quite similar but remember, the grey seal is more closely related to the brown bear than the family pet. An adult Labrador weighs no more than thirty five kilograms which as we already know is over

10 times less than the weight of an adult bull seal.

Never forget that these are wild animals and that you are diving in their backyard so always be respectful. Don't try to chase the seals, don't try to touch them until they invite you to do so and very importantly never approach the grey seal on land.

On land the grey seal is at its most vulnerable, the seals have to haul out to rest and to digest their food. When the seals are out of the water they should be left alone, this applies both around the islands and if you stumble across a seal hauled out on any beach. By all means observe from a distance but never approach a seal on land, don't try to haul them back into the sea to save them and don't be tempted to get yourself a seal selfie.

While the seal is hauled out it is vulnerable, it isn't designed for the land, in much the same way that we aren't designed for the water. It is now the seal that is hampered and cant move quickly, it is clumsy and restricted in its defences so will use the only weapon it possesses. The bite pressure of an adult bull is equivalent to that of the brown bear, even a young seal can give a very nasty bite, the seals mouth is also host to some pretty nasty bacteria which cause necrotising wounds requiring specialist antibiotics. The grey seal also has the ability to stretch out and twist its neck around to some seemingly impossible position's, at sea this is vital for catching fish, on land when provoked this also comes in handy for taking a lump out of a would be selfie taker so be warned!!

If you have any doubts about the health or welfare of a hauled out seal anywhere around the coast or even up the river systems and estuary's of the UK you can call the British Divers Marine Life Rescue (BDMLR) on 01825 765546 and they will send out a qualified medic to asses the seal and provide whatever help is needed.

This said, there is nothing like being in the water sharing time and space with these magnificent creatures and in this book I will explain to you how to get the most out of your time in the water.

The where.

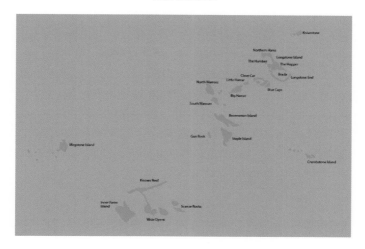

In the previous chapter I made the bold statement that the Farne Islands are quite simply the best place in the world to dive with grey seals. There are of course other places such as Lundy island and Anglesey where you will get good results by following the methods described in this book but for me and thousands of others you can never beat the Farnes for seal diving.

The islands lie just 2 miles from the harbour at Seahouses where a days diving can be booked on a charter boat through Billy Shiel Farne Island boat trips. Small boat launch is also available through the harbour office at Seahouses and from Beadnell boat launch at Beadnells main car park.

In the summertime the visibility around the islands can

reach up to twenty meters with ten meters being the norm. This is mainly due to the absence of major river run off on this stretch of the coast meaning that the is less sediment in the water to destroy the visibility. This said though a good easterly blow can soon reduce the viz to zero and scupper the diving completely for a few days, this is UK diving after all. The water temperature will reach around 15° C towards the end of August and into September but will fall as low as 5° C in March and April before steadily rising once again.

At low tide the Farne Islands are made up of 28 islands and exposed reefs, this number shrinks to 14 islands at high tide as the lower level islands and reefs are swamped by the incoming North Sea. Because of this, for the diver who visits the islands only once or twice a year the Farnes can look completely different on each visit with only the lighthouses and buildings remaining constant features.

The closest island to shore also happens to be the largest, Inner Farne is a little over one mile from the beach at Monkshouse and two miles from Seahouses harbour. Inner Farne is recognisable by its squat white lighthouse and 16th century Pele tower.

The island furthest out to sea is Knivestone, this is one of the islands that disappears as the tide rises making it one of the biggest shipwreck sites in the area. Knivestone lies approximately 5 miles from the harbour at Seahouses and just to the east of Longstone island which is easily recognisable by its famous red and white light house.

As well as the grey seals, divers will also be interested to know that the Farne Islands are the final resting place of several hundred shipwrecks, most of these are broken up and in most cases completely lost to the elements but there are still several wrecks that are well worth exploring. For more information on diving the wrecks of the Farne Islands the dive guides written by the late Ron Young are essential reading.

The islands are also home during the summer months to a huge seabird colony which include puffins, guillemots, razorbills, shags, cormorants, kittiwakes and fulmar as well as several species of tern. From April through to August the trip boats run by Billy Shiel Farne Island boat trips are packed with wildlife photographers and tourists heading out to see the seabirds up close.

Only two of the islands are open to the public, the rest of the Farne Islands are reserved strictly for the wildlife. Inner Farne and Staple island are open to the public during nesting season, they are owned and protected by the National Trust. They are well worth taking the time to visit during the summer months, walking amongst the puffins and being dive-bombed by Arctic Terns is the perfect way to announce that summer is here.

Tickets can be bought from the National Trust office at Seahouses harbour and the boat to get you out there can be booked through Billy Shiel Farne Island Boat Trips.

According to several wildlife photographers and film makers the Farne Islands are the closest thing to the

Galapagos that can be found in the northern hemisphere, I'm not sure how accurate that is but I do know that the Farne islands are very special place.

So where is the best place around the islands to dive with grey seals?

This all depends on the time of year.

The diving season officially starts in April but we dive the islands all year round, weather permitting. In April encounters with seals can be difficult. Most of the seals will be found around the outer islands, Longstone, Knivestone and Crumbstone being the most likely places to find them. As the season unfolds the seals start to colonise many of the other islands including Big Harcar, Little Harcar, the North and South Wamses and the Blue Caps. They can be unpredictable so any diving day starts with a seal hunt to see where the seals are lurking.

The tide and wind conditions also play a huge part in where we can dive safely with the seals. The tide in the this part of the North Sea floods South and ebbs to the North, when the tide comes in contact with the islands it is deflected around the rocks and the tides direction will change by the hour.

Generally speaking, when the tide is flooding its safe to dive to the South of the islands and when the tide ebbing its safe to dive to the North, the reason for this is that you don't want the tide pushing you on to the rocks as this makes it dangerous if not impossible for the boat to pick you up. We have to also consider the wind direction for the same reasons.

Because Of how the Farne Islands are located it is usually possible to dive the islands at any state of the tide, That isn't to say that the conditions will be suitable for diving with seals however.

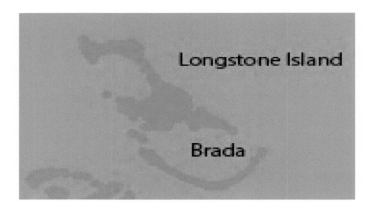

Consider this example.

On Longstone island there is a lagoon named Brada, this lagoon is a maximum of five to six meters deep on a high tide and for most of the year is possibly the best location for seal interactions. At low water on a spring tide however Brada can be almost empty of water and as such completely undivable.

If the wind is blowing from the East, North East or South East huge rolling waves will enter the mouth of Brada making it impossible to get a boat close to its mouth let alone drop divers in to safely dive it.

Planning and good fortune will always play the biggest part in any dive, especially when it comes to successful seal encounters.

Another element to take into consideration when planning a dive trip with grey seals is depth. Broadly speaking the Farne Islands sit on a twenty meter plateau of dolerite known as the great Whin sill. This is the same piece of rock that Bamburgh castle sits on and it extends inland under Hadrian s wall and all the way back as far as the Pennines.

On the South edge of the islands the cliffs descend steeply into the depths providing good wall dives, while to the North the islands slope gradually into the depths.

The best seal interactions happen at depths of between five and ten meters and its usually best practice to find a good spot on the sea bed to wait for the seals. For those that are new to seal diving the North side of the islands (with one or two exceptions) can be the best place to start.

This isn't always the case however, but it does take a lot of the stress of maintaining buoyancy control and depth awareness away from the diver that is new to seal diving once the excitement begins.

I've had several good interactions on much deeper dives but these tend to be more by chance than by planning. Once on the Chris Christiansen wreck I was mobbed by three adult female grey seals while still on the descent line at 30m. It was impossible and unsafe for me to continue the wreck dive while being assaulted from all directions so a quick plan "B" was devised and I spent my entire dive playing with the seals while slowly making my way back up the line, this is unusual behaviour at such a depth but not unheard of especially in September and October.

So far we have mainly covered "The where" from topside so now its time to get wet, we've found a site with favourable tides and wind direction. There are plenty of seals in the water and we know that we want to set up camp in between five and ten meters of water. But where is good to set up camp and wait?

Kelp is good, Grey seals are ambush predators, they like to sneak up on their prey and they also like a good old game of peekaboo so kelp can be a very good place to get some close encounters.

Kelp that has been flattened is usually a good place to find pregnant cow seals resting on the bottom.

Gullies and crevices, the seals use many hidden tunnels and narrow gullies to get around, many of the gullies are hidden just below the kelp and these are great places to watch the seals as they fly by at full speed.

You will often find mature cow seals sleeping in cracks and crevices out of the current, they will sometimes be lined up nose to tail along a crack in the rock, try not to disturb them but watch from a distance as they rise to the surface for a breath before sinking back down into their watery beds.

Sandy patches are perfect places for interactions, the seals use the sandy patches as scratching posts, they will drag their backs through the sand trying to scratch that elusive itch, a diver can sometimes come in handy when it comes to the really hard to reach ones.

Be patient, once you find a spot that looks suitable its time to settle down, sometimes the seals will appear immediately with a few fly pasts. Sometimes it will take longer and occasionally they will ignore you completely, don't give up though, give your spot a good twenty minutes and if nothings happening by then move along and try another.

In conclusion for "The where"

1. Find the seals

2. Is the wind and tide favourable?

3. Plan the dive to a maximum of ten meters and find a good spot to set up camp

The when.

Diving with grey seals is very season dependent, in order to ensure the best possible dive with seals you first have to understand how the seals year unfolds. As I mentioned earlier, September is the start of both breeding and pupping season, it continues through October, into November and December and is over by the start of January.

January through to April are very quiet times for the grey seals, the seals malt their winter coat to get ready for summer, there isn't much food in the water for them either so they spend a great deal of time out on the rocks, only entering the water when the tide is high enough to wash them off.

By May the grey seals are starting to enter the water and will spend a lot of time out hunting until the end of August. The summer months are the main time of year for the seals to fatten up so they will spend days at a time out at sea feeding and gaining the extra calories that are needed for the breeding season.

Some days during the summer months you won't see a single seal around the islands but when they are around the interactions can be very good.

September and October are without doubt the best times to dive with the grey seals, During pupping and breeding season the adult seals don't feed, this means that when the seals are in the water they have time to play, the young seals have an abundance of food which means that they also have plenty of time and energy for mischief.

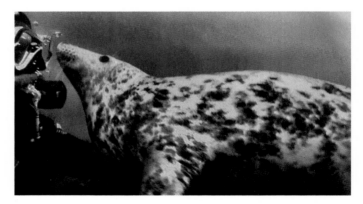

You will often see pregnant cow seals sleeping either on the seabed or wedged into cracks in the rocks and even wound around lobster pot lines to anchor them while they snooze. They do this partly for peace and quiet and partly because space on the rocks is at a premium at this time of year.

The grey seal can breath hold for up to twenty minutes. A Grey Seal sleeping on the seabed will stay down for fifteen to twenty minutes then slowly rise to the surface take a single breath and return to her place on the seabed. She may open her eyes to look around or they may remain closed. She can spend hours on end doing this, often for a full turn of the tide.

A good trick if you see a large female sleeping on the seabed is to settle down yourself at a distance that doesn't disturb her and watch. She will know that you're there and may watch you back for a while but will soon drift back into sleep. When she goes to the surface for her next breath she will either move away completely when she descends again in which case she should be left alone, more likely though she will settle down closer to the diver. If patience and air allow you should stay where you are ,breathing slowly and calmly and wait for the seal to go back to the surface for her next breath. After which she is likely to descend and settle down next to the diver. If this happens it's not unusual for the seal to scratch at the diver with her flipper which opens the door for one of the most intimate contacts a diver can have with a Grey Seal, the handhold. The seals flipper is very much like a hand and she is able to hold hands when she feels comfortable.

One of the most frustrating parts of planning a dive with grey seals is arriving at a dive site with perfect wind and tide conditions, tens or even hundreds of seals sunning themselves on the rocks but not a single seal in the water.

This comes down to planning.

The temptation is to scare the seals into the water either with the boat or by swimming up to the rocks, they want to play with us really so what's the harm?

When a seal becomes nervous it will head into the water where it feel safer, so yes you have achieved that part of the objective but a scared seal isn't going to pause to play with its tormentor and what's more when one or two seals panic and rush for the water mass hysteria affects the entire colony and the rest of them will follow.

This isn't a good situation for the diver as the seals have entered the water en mass in an agitated state and the unwitting diver has put himself between them and the safety of deep water.

Once again planning is the key to avoid this situation.

Grey seals are naturally lazy creatures, left to their own devices they will lay in the sun all day, scratching, farting and singing their haunting song. They allow the tides to rule their lives completely.

If you sit in boat for a full turn of the tide and watch the seals you will see what I mean. When the tide is high the seals will all be in the water hunting and playing, as the tide begins to ebb the seals will move in closer to the rocks and allow the tide to recede around them until they are left high and dry back on the rocks where they will stay until the tide rises high enough to wash them back off again.

This knowledge gives us an important tool to use when planning our dive with grey seals and helps us avoid arriving at a dive site with hundreds of seals on the rocks but none in the water. We simply plan our dive to coincide with when the tide is flooding, preferably near the top end of the flood tide or high water.

In conclusion for 'the when' section.

April is the start of the diving season. The grey seals will be mainly found around the outer islands, Knivestone, Longstone and Crumbstone being the most likely places to find them.

By June many of the seals will have moved to Big Harcar, Little Harcar, the Blue Caps and North Wamses. But from June through to the end of August the seals will be scarce as they are busy hunting and fattening up for the breeding season.

In September and October the grey seals will have colonised all of the outer islands, the seabed and the nooks and crannies in the reef walls. The first of the Pups will have been born and breeding season will be in full swing, this is the best time to dive with the seals.

The breeding and pupping season will continue through November into December and as space becomes harder to find the seals will start to colonise the inner group of the islands.

Its rare for divers to dive the inner group of the Farnes, this is partly because of all the trip boats heading out from Seahouses but mainly because the seals will stay out around the outer group until November/ December time by which time the diving season is over for all but the hardiest souls.

January through to April at the hardest months to get interactions with the seals as they spend as much time as possible out of the water, they go through their annual moult during this period and the new seal pups have mostly gone out to sea.

The how.

So now that we know "the What, the When and the Where" is going to give us our best chance of interactions with grey seals we need to know the little tips and tricks that can give us the best chance of interaction.

The first and most important of these tips is patience, always remember that when dealing with wild animals and nature whether we are underwater, in a forest or on a mountain side patience is key.

All animals large and small rely completely on their fight or flight mechanism, in a nutshell this means that in order to be accepted in the environment of a wild animal that animal has to first become used to your presence. As a rule in the underwater world we don't have to wait long, staying still, in one place, breathing slowly and evenly a diver will become a part of the environment within around 15 minutes. Underwater photographers already understand this, it's amazing how much life emerges from a reef once the diver becomes a part of the natural environment.

So step one of your dive plan is to descend to the sea bed at around five meters and find a suitable spot to make camp and wait. Suitable spots include sandy patches where the seals like to come down for a scratch, crevices and swim throughs in the rock and seabed are also good places. The underwater photographer may wish to position themselves with a scenic backdrop to get the best photo opportunities, although this will backfire nine times out of ten as the seal will always approach from the least picturesque angle!!

The second tip relates to the fact that the grey seal usually makes first contact from behind, biting the divers fins and investigating any interesting equipment that happens to be hanging loose.

To make the most of this little gem of information, once you have found a suitable spot on the sea bed settle down facing your buddy, that way any seal interaction happening behind either you or your buddy will be seen by the other. Its worth adding a few communication signals to your dive plan relating to this and try to avoid the temptation to turn around immediately if your the lucky one getting nibbled.

Instead let your buddy watch and maybe film the interaction while you gently kick and scull your fins as the seal gets absorbed in hunting them, after five minutes or so if the seal hasn't decided to investigate you further try rolling onto your back and continue with the sculling. This is also a good time to try the fish hand technique described later.

I've filmed many divers swimming along reefs followed by several seals who swear after the dive that they saw no seals and had absolutely no contact. These divers are then gobsmacked when I show them the footage of the carnage going on behind them. The grey seals are such good stalkers that it is possible to enjoy a good wreck or wall dive and not see a single seal, that isn't to say that they aren't there. I've lost count of the amount of times I have been exploring a new dive site around the islands and turned around only to be faced by a startled grey face belonging to a seal who had been merrily following me around the reef. Often when I dive in Brada I place my go pro on a selfy stick and film myself as I swim along, the footage of seals following along behind me is still always surprising.

The grey seal is a curious and playful creature and will be attracted to anything out of the ordinary, a dome port on an underwater camera will mesmerise them, the bubbles exhaled by a diver are fascinating, the movement of the divers fins is irresistible and even stacking pebbles on the seabed will grab their attention. When nothing else is working do something unusual, hand stands, bubble rings, play catch the pebble with your buddy... the list is endless.

The grey seal relies heavily on its whiskers.

The whiskers are extremely sensitive to movement in the water, a Grey Seal can home in on a single fish from a hundred meters away using only is whiskers. This means that a Grey Seal that is completely blind can still hunt and fend for itself. This is thought to be the main reason that the grey seals are attracted to divers fins. It isn't the actual fin that attracts the seal, its the vortex that the fin creates as it is pushed though the water that initially attracts them, only then do the pretty colours cinch the deal.

This is another thing that we can use in our favour when trying to get interactions, try raising your legs in the air either laid on your back if you've found a good sandy patch or try a handstand if the seabed is rock or kelp and kick your fins. sculling and flutter kicks work well, both can be a good way to attract the seals, alternately and less ungainly the diver can mimic the fin action with the hands.

Practice makes perfect on this one though, start by putting your arm straight out in front and simply raise it up and down like a standard fin kick, slowly alter the movement to mimic a flutter kick and even the movement of a fish. Use the entire arm, the forearm, the hand alone by flexing the wrist and the fingers. Wiggle your fingers and combine several of the above, keep practising and altering the movements and you will soon become a fish hands master!!

Fish hands is a great technique for getting the seals to approach from the front, everyone has their own version and its just a case of practising on every seal dive. Remember its the vortex that the movement sends off that will initially attract the seal so a combination of forceful down strokes and quick finger flicks can work well on one dive where gentle side strokes might work better on the next.

An important thing to remember when using this technique is that at some stage the seal will come to investigate and that fingers and seal teeth are not a good combination!! simply curl your fingers into a fist and voila you have your first fist bump.

Sound can be a good tactic when it comes to the adult cow seals, mimicking the bull seal grunt is one technique that can work well, I also find that humming a tune and doing dolphin impressions (no matter how badly) also works well.

Eye contact, the grey seal is a predator but is also a prey animal to the Orca so the fight or flight mechanism is strong, underwater photographers look at life through a lens and always get the seals approaching head on way before divers who dive without cameras. This is because of eye contact, or in this case the absence of eye contact.

Once a seals trust has been established, eye contact isn't a problem and you can stare lovingly into its eyes to your hearts content but during the initial contact and establishing that trust eye contact is to be avoided.

Pregnant cow seals can often be found sleeping either on the sea bed or wedged into cracks in the rock face, the seals like to rip up and flatten areas of kelp and settle down for a snooze, you can try the technique described earlier in the book to interact with these ladies. Settle down at a respectful distance and wait to see how she reacts, if done right the interaction will be very peaceful and calming, a little bit like snuggling up on the sofa with your favourite dog.

On the other hand if you decide to ignore the advised method of approach and disturb the seal while she's sleeping you will still get a reaction but the interaction that you get will be anything but peaceful and will certainly not be calming.

Always remember that these are wild animals and it is unfair as well as potentially dangerous to assume that they want to play when they are clearly resting.

Disturb sleeping pregnant females of any species including human at your peril, you have been warned!!

Occasionally an adult bull seal will come along to check you out, they rarely try to interact but when they do it can be quite intimidating and my best advice to the diver who is new to this kind of diving is to swim away and find a different area to continue your dive.

If on the other hand you decide to see where the encounter leads it can be quite interesting, a bull seal tugging at your fins can have you flailing around like a rag doll and can result in the loss of a good fin.

I've had a bull seal bite through my DSMB and then come down to put its mouth around my thigh for what was luckily for me a gentle squeeze and yes my thigh fit easily between those sharp powerful jaws.

I've been pulled backwards through the water by a bull seal and I've been stuck face to face in a narrow passage where neither the bull nor I could pass each other.

All of these situations were intimidating and scary in some of them I did think that things might end badly but they didn't and to this day I've never been harmed by a bull seal.

Conclusion and dive planning

So now that we know "the What, the Where, the When and the How" lets put it all together and plan a dive with grey seals.

There are a few tools needed for this part, the first being an up to date tide timetable for Seahouses or North Sunderland to give it its true name. There are several apps available for tide timetables , tides near me being one of the most popular, these usually only give you a seven day forecast however and if we are travelling to the Farnes and want to plan our dive trip properly we need to be looking at the tables several months in advance.

Imray do a fantastic app for this, you can check the tides up to twelve months in advance. You can check the tides at all of your favourite harbours around the UK and it provides good tidal curves as well as many other great features, it is a subscription app but only costs around £4 per year.

Alternatively tide tables are available at the Seahouses harbour office and the lifeboat station.

The weather and wind isn't something that we can check months in advance but it is vital to check it in the days leading up to your dive trip, the met office app is my go to weather app but there are several alternatives available too.

The third tool that we need is a tide atlas, the tide atlas is used in conjunction with the tide tables so that we can predict which direction the tide will be running and how quickly at any time from high water to low water and back to high water again.

The Farne islands are unusual in that the tide which runs North while ebbing and South while flooding gets deflected around the rocks in all directions and sometimes in two directions at once. For this reason I've included a custom tide atlas that shows these tidal direction changes.

To use the tidal atlas you first need to find high water for the day you want to dive on your tide table app. The lead up to high water is when there will be the most seals in the water so aim to plan dive one for two to three hours before high water and dive two for either one hour before or right on high water, this will allow a one hour surface interval and two one hour dives.

We now need to look at the tide atlas for suitable areas to dive, we pick several spots to check out on the day of the dive as the seals may not be in the area which we've prioritised so plan B, C and D are all valid.

This all looks nice and simple until we check the tide tables for our intended dates for the dive trip and find that high water is at 7am and 7pm and we cant find a skipper to take us diving at 3am or miss his supper by going out diving until 9pm.

So best practice is to study the tide tables first then book the trip for the dates where high tide falls around lunchtime, unless your bringing your own boat of course, in which case enjoy your 3am start.

The following maps show the general areas that the seals can be found throughout the year, these spots are highlighted in blue.

The red highlights indicate the best spots for seal diving

January

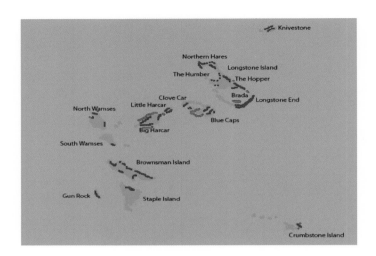

February

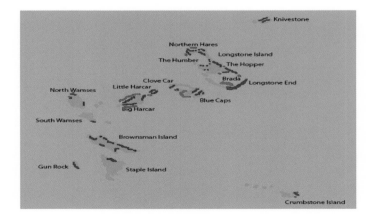

March

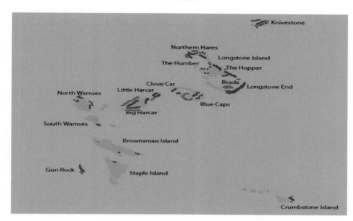

April and May

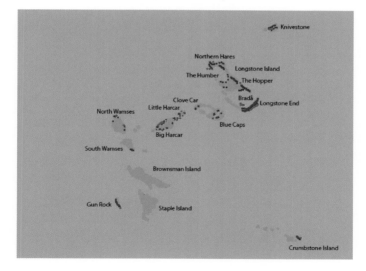

June, July and August

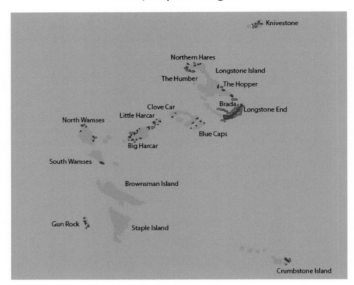

September and October

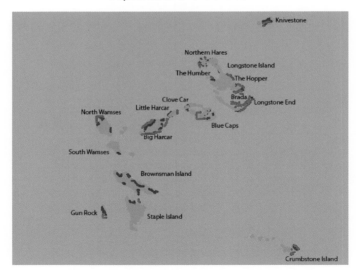

November and December

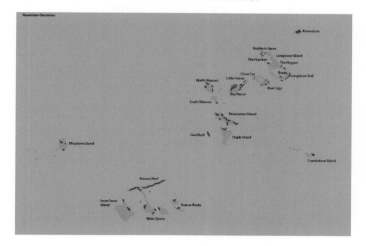

The Farne Islands Tide Atlas

The tide Atlas is to be used alongside up to date tide tables which are available to purchase from the harbour office and lifeboat station at Seahouses. I personally use the Imray tides app, its an annual subscription and also includes a good UK tide atlas which is handy for assessing the speed and direction of the main tidal stream.

Together with the maps on the previous pages and up to date weather information these tools can be used to find the safest and most productive spots to dive with grey seals.

These tools are in no way to be considered foolproof and are in no way a substitute for local knowledge, always take advice from your skipper and if the conditions don't look safe then don't be afraid to call the dive.

The author takes no responsibility for the incorrect use of the tools provided and assumes that the reader intending to use these tools is a qualified scuba diver and has a basic knowledge of tides and currents or is lasing with a skipper who does.

There are thirteen maps in the tide timetable starting with high water (HW) there are six hour by hour maps showing the general direction of tides after high water (+HW) and six maps showing the general direction of tides before high water (-HW) these maps are not to be used for navigation and are not a substitute for a UK tide Atlas, the maps are intended to show how the direction of tide is affected by the Farne Islands

By finding high water on your tide timetable for any given date you can move forward and backwards to cross reference these maps to find the most suitable spots to dive with seals.

To make things even easier I have listed the most suitable spots to dive as a footnote to each map.

Don't forget to make allowances for the weather, especially the wind direction and strength and if in doubt check everything over with the skipper before committing to the dive plan.

High water +6 hours

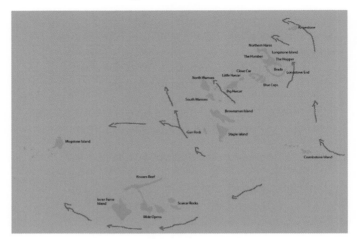

The tide is low and is ebbing n a northerly direction, you can see how the direction of tide is affected by the islands.

This is a good time to view seals on the rocks but not a good time to dive with them.

The best options for dive sites are the Hopper and the North side of Big Harcar

The Hopper is a gulley on the east side of Longstone island, its easily recognisable by the Hopper rock which stands taller than any other on the island, the gulley is to the south of the rock, the depth is between 14 and 18 meters but despite this the hopper can be one of the best spots for interactions

High water +5 hours

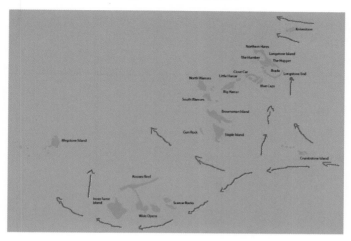

The tide is ebbing to the north

The best options for dive sites are the Hopper and the north side of Big Harcar,

The north side of Big Harcar slopes out on a steady gradient from the island to the seabed at around 12 meters so is a good place for new seal divers as you can chose a spot in a suitable depth to wait, one thing to be aware of with this site is not to go too far west as the pull is very strong at that end of the island as the tide gets funnelled through Piper Gut.

High water +4 hours

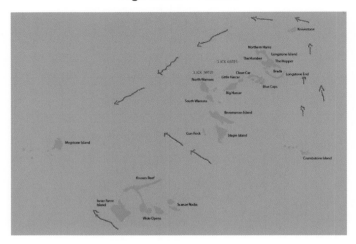

The tide is ebbing to the north

Our dive site options are very limited only the north side of Big Harcar and Northern Hares available

Northern Hares is located at the north of Longstone island, the best spot for seals being on the north west corner of the island, its a shallow site but can be good for interactions.

High water +3 hours

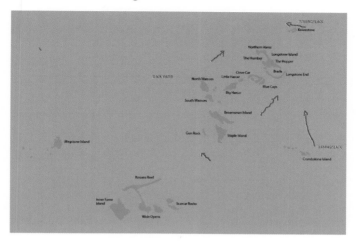

The tide is beginning to ebb to the north

Our options for dive sites are the Hopper, Big Harcar (north side) and Northern Hares.

Depending on the time of year you could also try the north side of Megstone

The north side of Megstone has a small gulley which can be good for interactions , you can see the gulley from the surface as a split in the rock, there are often seals around this part of the Megstone even when the rest of the islands are bare.

High water +2 hours

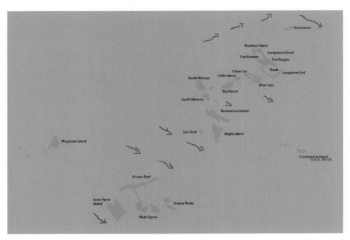

Although we are 2 hours past high water the tide is still in flood so is heading south, this gives us a wider choice of dive sites but many of the seals will already be out of the water. Brada would be my first choice for seals

Swimming into Brada with the Longstone end wall on your left you will find a combination of sand patches and kelp forest in a depth of around 5 meters, Brada is without doubt the best place around the Farnes for seal interactions, there are gulleys and kelp forests further to the north but the best place for seals is to the south west of the lagoon.

Crumbstones east side would be second, there can be hundreds of seals in the water around the south east corner of Crumbstone, its kelpy and surrounded by strong tides and currents making it hard to move very far but the seal interactions can be fantastic.

The Hopper, north side of Big Harcar and North Wamses are also good options

High water +1 hour

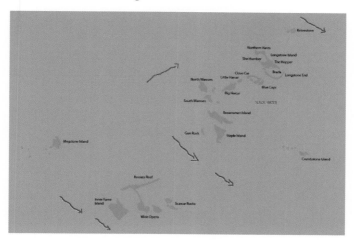

The tide is flooding to the south and there should be plenty of seals in the water .

Brada, The Hopper, Bluecaps, Little Harcar and Big Harcar (south side) are all good options , in the winter its also worth looking in Pinnacles Gut, as the seals start to colonise the bigger islands during pupping season. The Pinnacles Gut can be a good place to find the heavily pregnant cow seals, the gut is to the south of Staple and Brownsman islands in the narrow channel where the Brownsman landing jetty is located.

High water at Seahouses

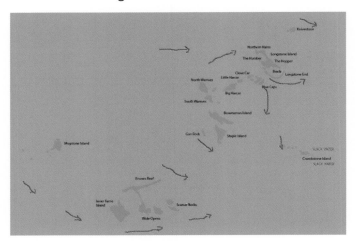

The tide is flooding to the south, the seals have been washed off of the rocks and are hopefully feeling playful

Brada, The Hopper, Bluecaps, Little Harcar and Big Harcar (south side) are all good options for dive sites

Big Harcar (south side) is a good wall dive with seals ranging along its length, there is a strong tidal pull at the west end at Piper Gut so care must be taken when diving this end, swimming south away from the rock will take you to around twenty meters but closer in you can chose your depth with five to ten meters being best for seals.

There is a gut between big and little harcar which can be fantastic for seal interactions, its popular with pregnant cow seals, in September and October you will find them sleeping on the bottom and wedged into the cracks in the rock to the west of the gut.

High water -1 hour

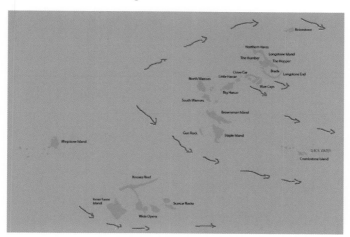

The tide is flooding to the south, the seals are in the water

Dive sites to consider are Brada, The Hopper, Bluecaps, Little Harcar and Big Harcar (south side)

Pinnacles gut is also an option in the winter months

Little Harcar is an interesting wall dive , enter at the east side of the rock where there are usually seals to be found, swim along the wall to the west into the gut between big and little harcar if the seals aren't playing on the east side.

High water -2 hours

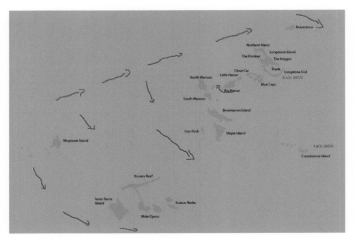

The tide is flooding and there will be seals in the water.

Brada, Bluecaps, Little and Big Harcar (south side) are the best options for dive sites

High water -3 hours

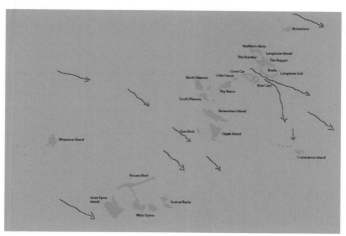

The tide is beginning to flood in a southerly direction, were a little early for seal diving yet but you may get lucky around Bluecaps, the best place to start is the gulley on the east side of Bluecaps, the gulley splits the reef and although it gets shallow in places it is well worth exploring , don't be surprised when you turn to head back out if there is an inquisitive seal hot on your heels, keep the wall on your right as you exit and follow the reef around to find a suitable spot to await your prey.

Little Harcar and Big Harcar on the south side are other options for this state of tide.

High water -4 hours

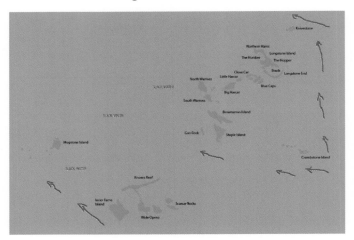

The ebb tide is never the best time to dive with grey seals but the place to try at this state of tide is Longstone end, this is a stunning dive site, part boulder field and part wall with gullies and cracks to explore, the site is full of life including octopus and squat lobster, even if the seals don't come and play this is a good dive.

Other options are Big and Little Harcar (south side)

High water -5 hours

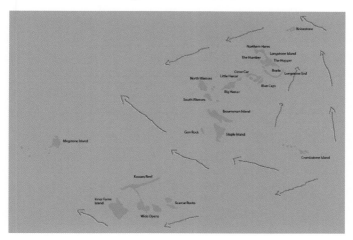

The tide is ebbing to the north and the seals will be mostly high and dry on the rocks.

The Knivestone would be my choice at this state of tide, ask your skipper to drop you at the east side of the island at the mouth of the gulley that splits the island , its a shallow swim through but can be excellent for seals, the gulley opens up on the west side and drops down to around fourteen meters where you will find the scattered wreckage of the Abyssinia which is a great plan B if the seals aren't playing.

Other sites to consider at this state of tide are Gun Rock, Big Harcar (north side) and north Wamses

High water -6 hours

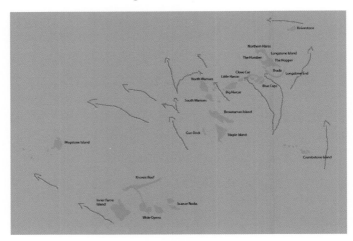

Low water ebb tide, even I would struggle to find a seal at this state of tide, the north side of Big Harcar is really your only hope.

So there we have it.

The what, the where, the when and the how to dive with grey seals.

I hope that this book has given you plenty of tips and tricks for getting the most out of your next trip to the Farne islands.

Remember to plan well in advance to ensure getting into the water at the best possible time to not only get the best possible chance of interaction but also to be able to dive the sites that you want to see.

I highly recommend the Imray app for tides and tide atlas not only for the Farnes but for planning your dive trips anywhere around the UK.

I use the met office app for weather and if you want to take things a stage further when dive planning there are always admiralty charts to sink your teeth into.

Thanks you for buying the book.

Please follow on twitter @divethefarnes

Facebook @softencounters

Dive safe.

Steve.

Printed in Great Britain
by Amazon